The Little Blue Manuscript Book

Hello! I'm Tap, the music firefly.
Have fun writing your own music in this book!

This manuscript book belongs to:

Notes and Rests

Quarter Note

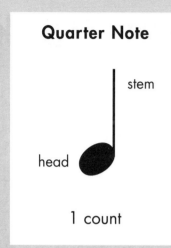

1 count

Half Note

2 counts

Dotted Half Note

3 counts

Whole Note

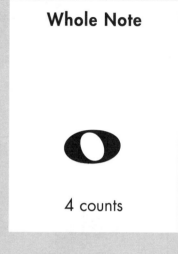

4 counts

Stem Direction

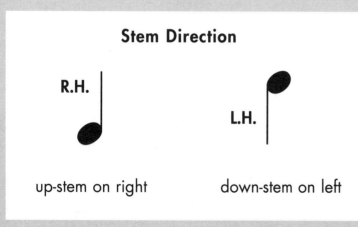

up-stem on right   down-stem on left

Quarter Rest

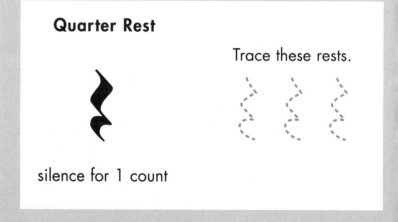

silence for 1 count

Trace these rests.

The Measure

In music, the notes are grouped into **measures**.
Each measure has the same number of counts (beats).
Bar lines divide the music into measures.

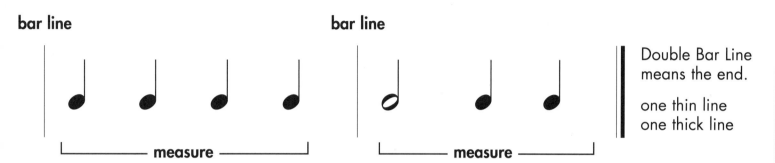

bar line   bar line

Double Bar Line
means the end.

one thin line
one thick line

measure   measure

Time Signature

The **time signature** is two numbers at the beginning of the music.

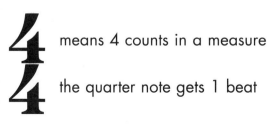 means 4 counts in a measure

the quarter note gets 1 beat

 means 3 counts in a measure

the quarter note gets 1 beat

The Staff

This is a staff. It has 5 lines and 4 spaces.

Notes are written **on the lines** or **in the spaces** of the staff.

Line Notes

Space Notes

The Grand Staff

In piano music we use two staffs. Together we call them the **grand staff**.

Complete these grand staffs by adding the bar line and tracing the brace.

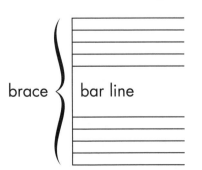

brace

bar line

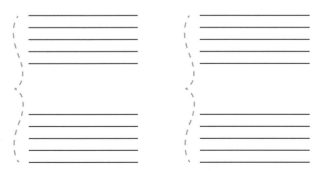

Bass Clef

This is a **bass clef**. Bass means *low* sounds.

The bass clef is placed on the bottom staff. It shows notes BELOW Middle C.

The left hand usually plays the bass notes.

L.H.

Treble Clef

This is a **treble clef**. Treble means *high* sounds.

The treble clef is placed on the top staff. It shows notes ABOVE Middle C.

The right hand usually plays the treble notes.

R.H.

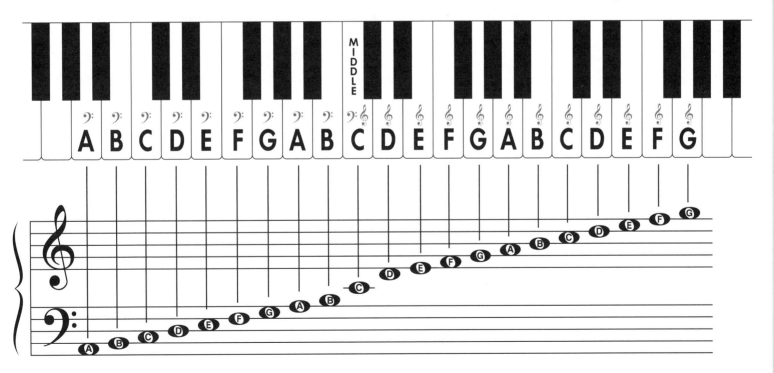

Drawing the Treble Clef

Treble clefs are fun to draw. Follow these steps.

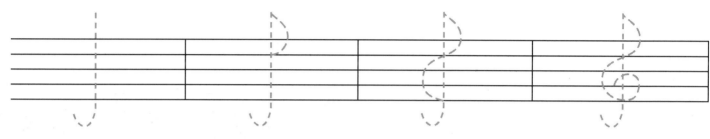

Draw a candy cane or "J." Make it begin above the staff and curve below line 1.

Draw a half-circle that crosses at line 4.

Swing to the left and curve down to line 1.

Curl around line 2.

Now draw four treble clefs on your own.

Drawing the Bass Clef 𝄢

Bass clefs are also fun to draw. Imitate each step below.

Draw a large dot on line 2 (counting down).

Draw a curving line to the right. Go to the top of the staff and then down to the bottom.

Draw two dots above and below line 2 (counting down).

Now draw four bass clefs on your own.

Writing in 4/4 Time

You can compose music in 4/4 time! Follow these steps to complete your piece.

1. Complete the grand staff by tracing the bar line and brace.
2. Trace the clefs, time signature, and bar lines.
3. Fill each measure with one of the sample rhythm patterns shown here.

Sample Rhythm Patterns

Writing in ¾ Time

You can also compose music in 3/4 time! Follow these steps to complete your piece.

1. Complete the grand staff by tracing the bar line and brace.
2. Trace the clefs, time signature, and bar lines.
3. Fill each measure with one of the sample rhythm patterns shown here.

Sample Rhythm Patterns

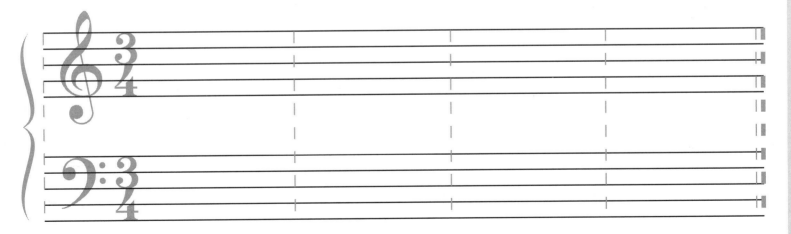

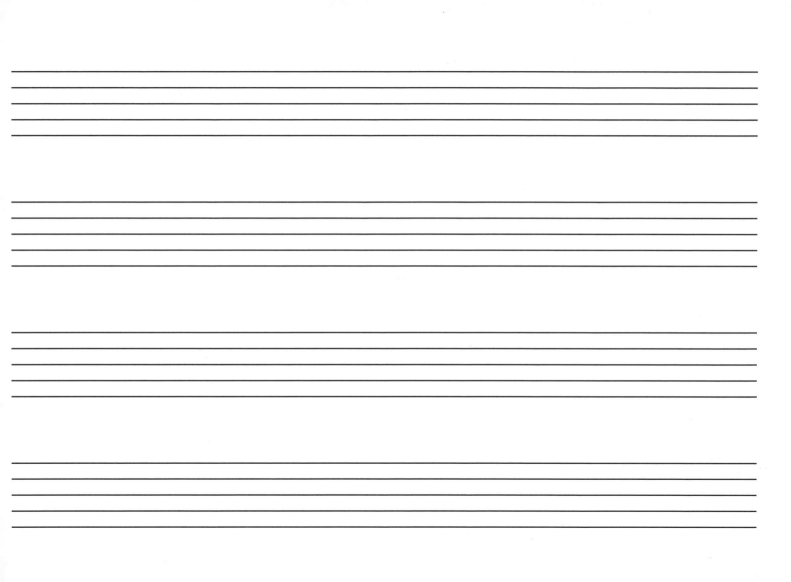

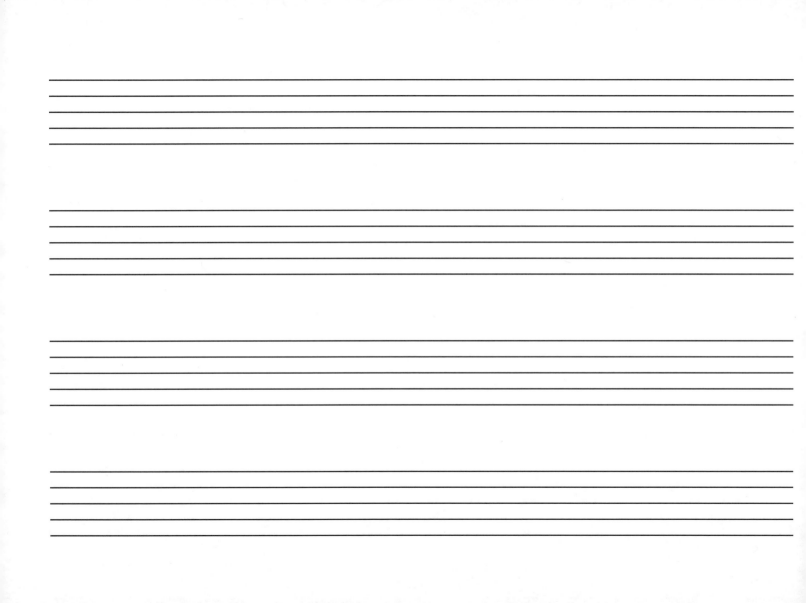

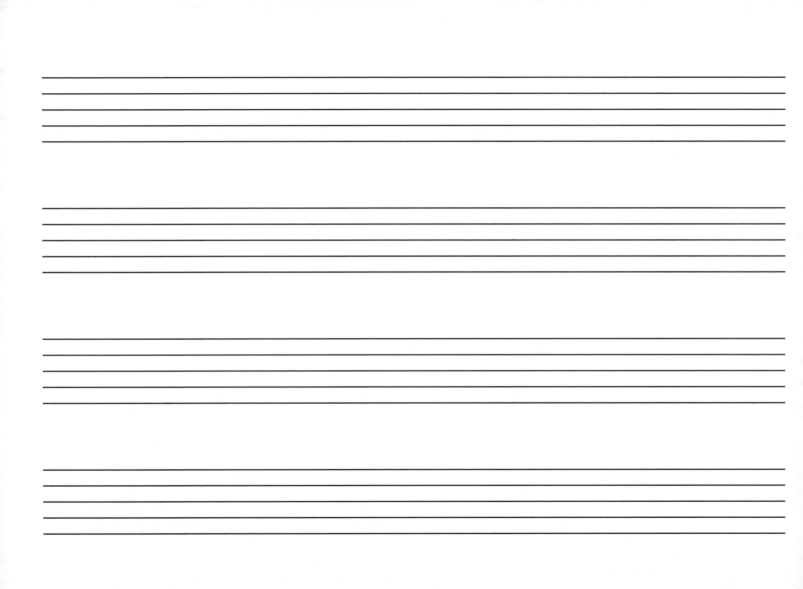

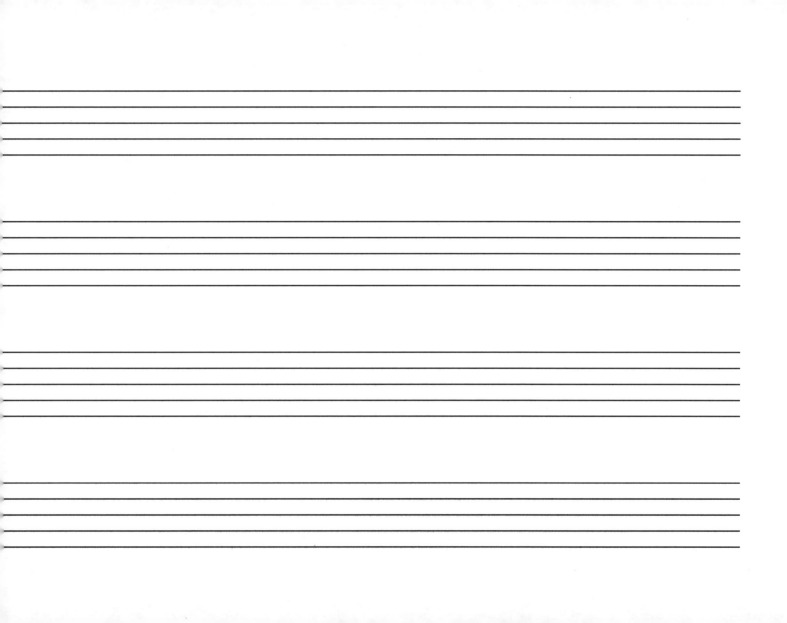

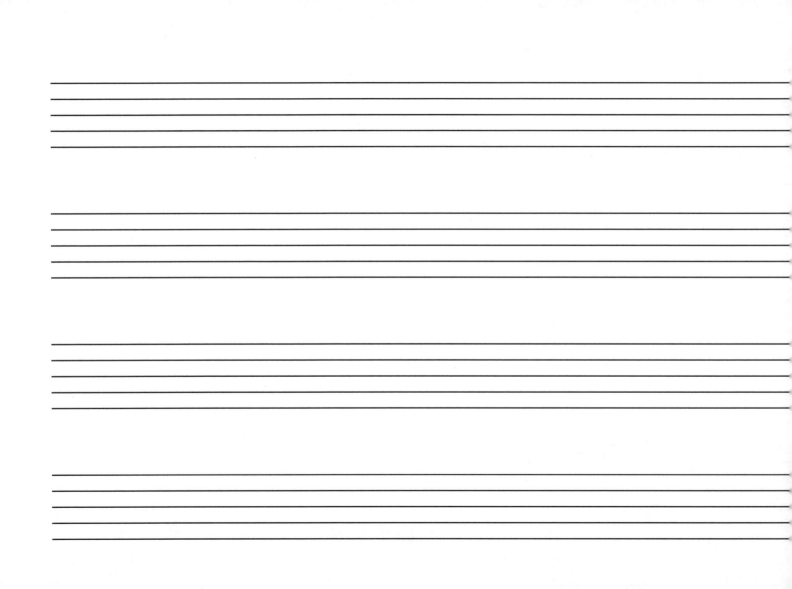

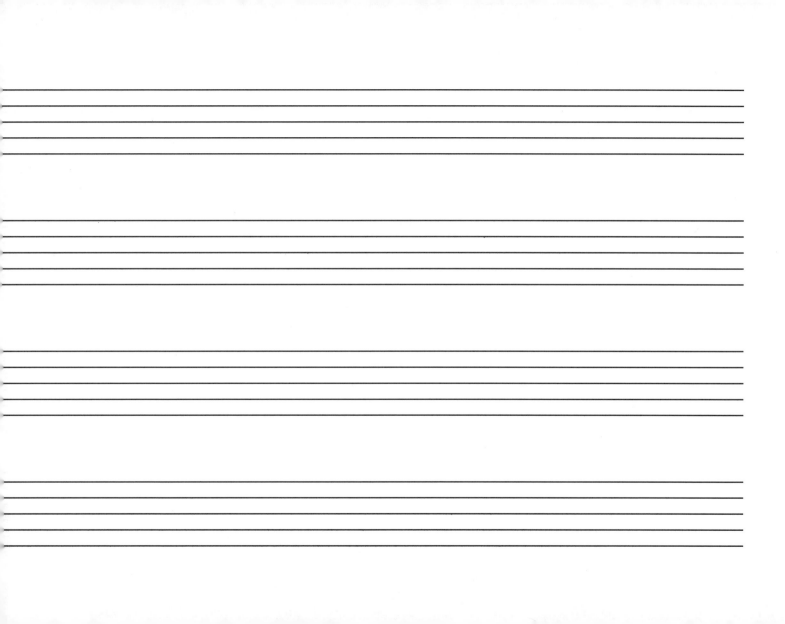

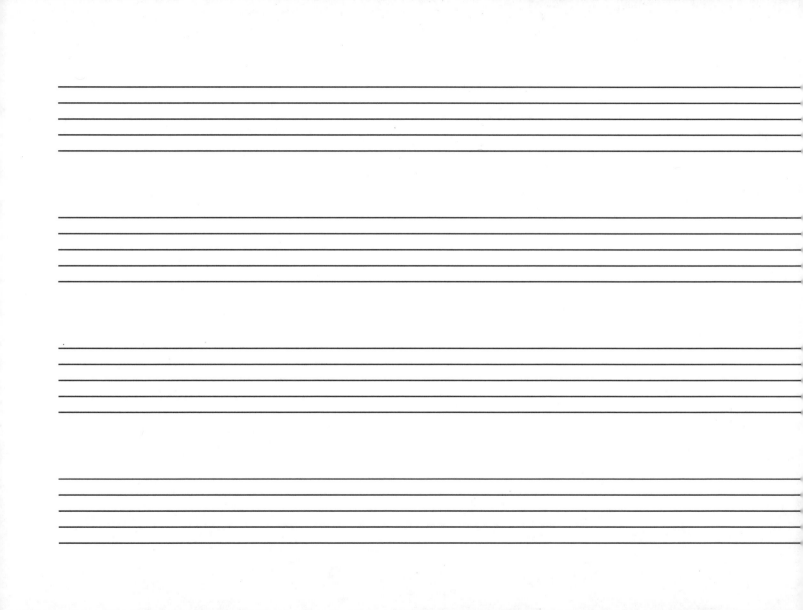

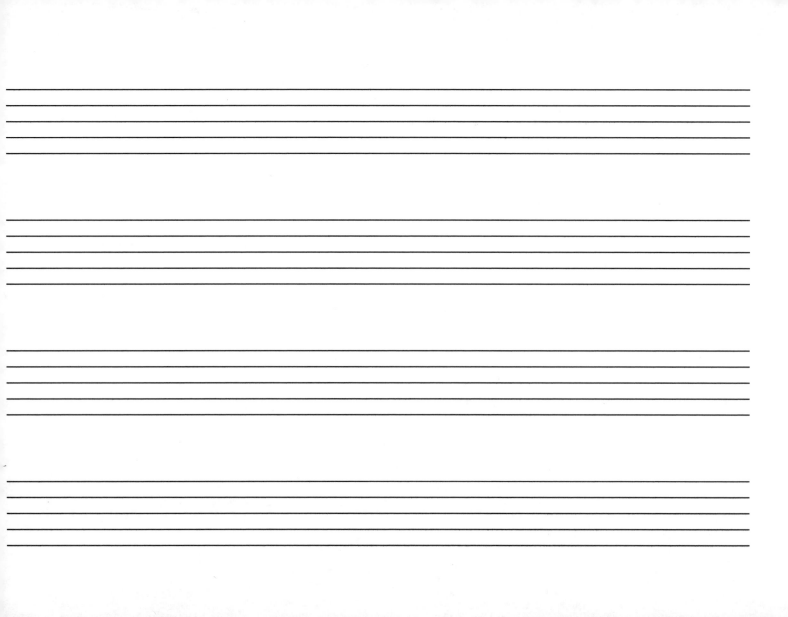

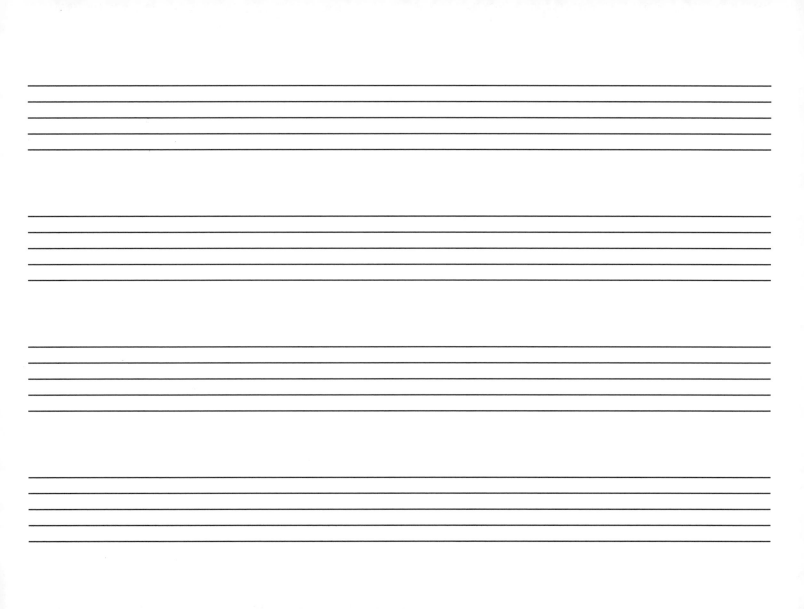

Ideas for the Teacher

The following are sample ideas for use at the lesson or at-home assignment.

1. Have the student draw **treble clefs**, **bass clefs**, and form **grand staffs** with a bar line and brace.

2. Student **names** a set of notes that the teacher writes.

3. Student **copies** a set of notes that the teacher draws, then names the notes.

Teacher draws.

Student copies exactly.

4. Student **copies a rhythm** the teacher draws, then writes the counts.